CODEMASTER #2

How to Write and Decode
More Top-Secret Messages

CODEMASTER #2 ®

How to Write and Decode
More Top-Secret Messages

SCHOLASTIC INC.

New York Toronto London Auckland Sydney
Mexico City New Delhi Hong Kong Buenos Aires

Art by Jim Frazier

ISBN 0-439-76119-0

12 11 10 9 8 7 6 5   10/0

Printed in the U.S.A.   40

First Scholastic book club printing, February 2005

For

6482359184, 822291326384, and 93646393

(Brown Fox Code)

Contents

CODEMASTER #2

How to Write and Decode
More Top-Secret Messages

Introduction

S*hhh!* Want to learn a big secret? Even better, do you want to learn how to keep all your secrets safe?

This book will show you lots of different ways to write secret messages. You can post your coded messages on a bulletin board, send them to friends, or use a code to make notes in your personal diary.

Most of the time when people talk about codes they really mean ciphers. Ciphers are a special kind of secret writing in which the words and letters have been shuffled, twisted, or disguised in all sorts of ways. In this book, the word *code* is used to mean *cipher*.

Before you start reading about codes, here is one word of warning. Be sure to hide this code book in a *very* safe place. Only you and your special friends should know its secrets. After all, you wouldn't want a curious spy snoop to discover it!

OK, Codemaster. Get ready to learn more secret codes.

And remember, *shhh*. It's a secret!

The List Code

Suppose you have a club and need to post a special announcement for all your club members. But you don't want any outsiders to know what it says.

Where would you put the secret message? And how would you disguise it? Easy! You can put your message in clear view if you use the list code.

A list code can be a list of just about anything, as long as it has a number next to each item. It could be a shopping list, a tally of

3

hours per week spent watching television, or money earned from baby-sitting or doing odd jobs. In this sample, it's a list of all the members of your club with the number of books each person read during the semester.

SUPER READERS CLUB	
TOM	13
SPENCER	16
GREG	13
SCOTT	15
OLIVER	11
DONNA	14
SETH	11
AUDREY	12
RANDY	13
DOUG	11
MATT	12
TROY	14

Post the list in a place where all your friends can see it—on a bulletin board at school, for instance. They will quickly figure out what it means. It tells them the day of your next clubhouse meeting.

How does the list code work? Its secret is hidden in the numbers.

The last digit of the number next to each person's name is an important one. The first digit is a fake.

Start at the top of the list. The number for Tom is 13, so the number you are looking for is 3. Count to the third letter in Tom's name. It is the letter **M**. **M** is therefore the first letter in the secret announcement.

Let's look at Spencer's record. He seems to have read 16 books. His name is the code for the next letter in the announcement. It is an **E** (since the sixth letter in his name is **E**).

Now that you have the hang of it, unscramble the whole list code message.

The announcement says:

MEET ON SUNDAY

The list code is useful for announcements, such as **TOM HAS TICKETS**. You also can share helpful information, such as **BRING A SWEATER**, or you can tell your friends about a good book you have read.

MYSTERY BOOK

Here is the name of a fascinating book disguised using the list code. Can you figure out the title?

SUPER READERS CLUB	
SPENCER	11
SCOTT	12
TOM	12
AUDREY	14
TIPPER	14
OLIVER	13
DONNA	12
RANDY	13
GREG	10
SETH	11

For long messages, you can add fake names to your club list. But be careful; a spy might get suspicious. He'll wonder how all those people can fit in your clubhouse!

The book is *Scorpions* by Walter Dean Myers.

PASSPORT SECRETS

During the 1650s, Louis XIV of France invented a smart way to signal information about persons visiting his country. Each visitor was supplied with a letter of introduction from the king.

But hidden in the letter was a secret code giving information about the person who carried it.

The person's country of origin was shown by the color of the paper. His age was shown by its shape. Lines placed under the name told his height.

The length of a ribbon threaded through the top of the paper showed whether the person was married. And an ornamental scroll around the border meant he was rich.

Other marks described whether he was honest, stubborn, or intelligent.

So without a word being spoken, a person knowing the code could learn a lot about the unsuspecting stranger. And it was a perfect way to trap a spy who carried a letter stolen from someone else.

The Window Card Code

When you need to disguise a long message, the window card is a handy code. It works just like a secret code machine.

Use the example of a window code decoder on the next page to make one of your own. Trace it onto a piece of paper (if you want it to be extra strong, then trace it onto a piece of lightweight cardboard), and have an adult cut out the "windows."

Now you are ready to write a secret message. Take a blank sheet of paper and place the decoder card with the slanted corner at the *upper left*. Trace around the window card. You now have an outline of the card. When you lay the card over the outline, six holes show through.

Suppose you want to code a 12-word message: **I WILL MEET YOU AFTER CLASS AT THE CORNER OF ELM STREET**.

First print the first six words inside the openings as shown:

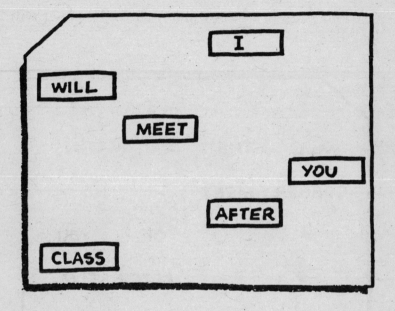

Now turn the card so the slanted corner is at the *lower right*. Six new openings are under the holes. Print the next six words inside them.

When you lift up the window card, the paper will look like this:

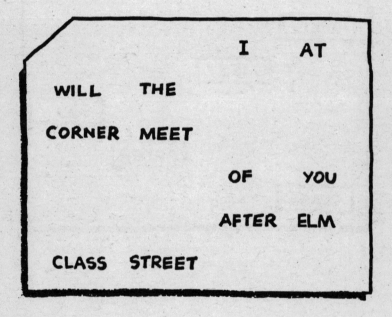

Disguise the secret writing even further. Fill in the blank spaces with 12 fake words that have nothing to do with your message:

SAM	WHY	I	AT
WILL	THE	ADAMS	DON'T
CORNER	MEET	YOU	SPIDER
GET	TOM	OF	YOU
BIKE	A	AFTER	ELM
CLASS	STREET	PAPER	HORSE

Your secret message is now hidden among the fake words. Erase the outline. Now only your friend can read the message. She takes her copy of the window card decoder, lays it over the words, and writes down the message.

To make a copy of the window card:

- Trace your card onto a piece of lightweight cardboard. Be sure to trace all the windows.
- Ask an adult to cut out the windows with a razor tool or hobby knife.
- Then use scissors to cut around the outside lines.

You may use the window card to make even longer messages. After coding the first 12 words, flip the window card over so the back is faceup and the slanted corner is at the *upper right*. Print six more words.

Then turn the card so the slanted corner is at the *lower left*. Print another six words inside the holes. You can code up to 24 words with the window card.

If any holes remain unfilled, add an extra "signal" word. It tells your friend that she is at the end of the message. For example, you might use the signal word **SPIDER**. Then fill in the remaining blanks with fake words.

MYSTERY BOOK

Ready to unscramble a message? The title of a book is printed inside the message on page 11. To find it, place the slanted corner at the *upper right* and start decoding. Then continue decoding with the slanted corner at the *lower left*.

The window card code is fun. Only you and your friends can see through its secret!

You have just discovered the book title *Why Don't You Get a Horse, Sam Adams?* by Jean Fritz.

THE TRICKY HARD-BOILED EGG

Secret messages have been passed through enemy lines in amazing ways. Here is one example from World War I.

The spy was a simple countrywoman carrying a basket of eggs. But even after carefully being searched, she got the message through. How did she do it? It seems the basket of eggs was not as innocent as it looked.

After the woman reached her destination, she handed a hard-boiled egg to a fellow agent. When the agent peeled off the shell, he discovered secret writing inside on the white of the egg!

Getting the message inside was simple. The chemical alum was dissolved in vinegar and used as "ink" to write the message on the eggshell. When the words dried, they became invisible on the shell. The "ink" had passed through the shell and reappeared inside on the egg white.

Tricky, huh?

The Line Code

Take a close look at this diagram of a square with lines crossing it.

It's a simple design, right? But the diagram hides a clever secret. By using just a few of the lines, you can make any letter of the alphabet.

The diagram can be used to send hidden messages to your friends. Here is how the code works. First, number the diagram like this:

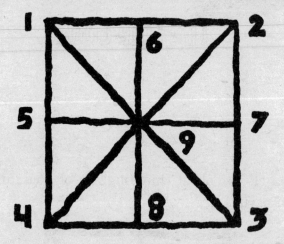

To make the letter **P**, draw a line from 4 to 1 to 2 to 7 to 5. The code number for the letter **P** is 41275. The letter **I** is drawn from 6 to 8 and is coded as 68. An **N** is 4132. The letters in the diagram look like this:

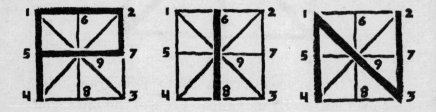

Just to be tricky, you can code the same letter in more than one way. For example, the letter **S** can be written as 215734 or 437512.

To draw line code letters such as **K**, you will need to lift your pencil. Use a comma to show the start of a new line. **K** is coded as 68,293. It looks like this when you draw it:

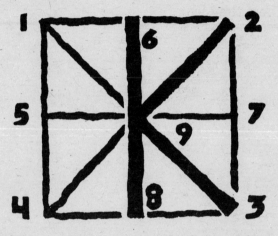

When you receive a secret message, place a piece of paper over the numbered diagram. Use the diagram as a guide to draw the first letter. Then shift the paper to the left and trace the next letter. Keep shifting. Before you know it, the full message appears on the paper!

Some line code letters take a little imagination to see. Here are some unusual-looking letters that will take some practice:

B = 921439
D = 1431
G = 214379
Q = 14321,39
V = 132

Grab a pencil and draw these letters in line code to see how they look.

Now that you have the idea, here is your chance for some line code practice. See if you can unscramble the title of this book:

215734 23412 1432

2314 1431 2143,57

41275,93

So the next time you see your friend, tell him you are going to drop him a line. He'll know exactly what you mean!

The answer is *Sounder* by William Armstrong.

The Ink Spot Code

Here is a "messy" code that is really "neat" to use. It's called the ink spot code because you can send a message written as smudgy spots. But when your friend deciphers it, your words are sharp and clear.

To prepare the ink spot code, print the letters of the alphabet in a row. The letters should be evenly spaced, so it may help to print them on graph paper. Leave about an inch between the left edge of the paper and the first letter:

Next, cut out the row of letters and paste it on a

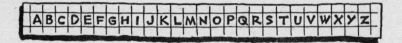

narrow strip of cardboard. This is your code strip. It can be used over and over again for heavy-duty message writing.

Write your ink spot code message on lined note-book paper. Suppose you want to send the message **PIZZA FOR LUNCH**. It sounds delicious!

To begin, lay the code strip just below the first line. Be sure the edge is even with the paper's left edge.

Now make a small ink spot directly above the letter **P** on your code strip.

Move the strip down to the next line, being careful that the code strip is still even with the paper's left edge. Then make your next ink spot above the **I**. The spot can be larger or smaller than the first; it really doesn't matter. The sloppier the better. The location of the spot is the key.

Move the code strip down to the next line for the third letter and the line below that for the fourth. Continue until you have "splattered" your secret message on the page. It will look like this:

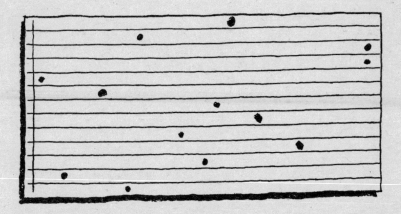

It looks kind of messy, doesn't it?

When your friend receives the message, he uses an identical code strip with the very same spacing.

Unscrambling the ink spot message is a snap. Your friend places his code strip below the first line, just the way you did. Then he slowly slides it down the page, one line at a time. On a separate piece of paper, he carefully writes down the code strip letter for each spot. Suddenly your entire message appears!

Are you ready for some practice? Get a piece of tracing paper and trace the code strip on page 20. Then test your code cracking skills to figure out the title of this book:

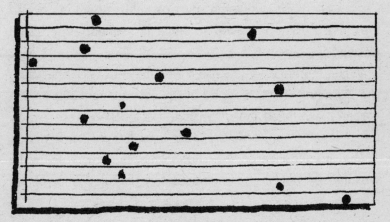

Use the ink spot code to write your very next secret message. And remember. Sloppiness counts!

Congratulations! You have just decoded *Freak the Mighty* by Rodman Philbrick.

THE SECRET OF THE DIRTY SHIRT

Years ago, a spy was in his hotel room in a foreign country. The enemy had posted agents to watch his every move. It seemed impossible for the spy to smuggle a secret message to his partner.

One afternoon, while the spy was in his room, he phoned the hotel desk and asked to have his soiled striped shirt cleaned.

When the maid left his room with the shirt under her arm, she was immediately stopped by the enemy agent outside. He carefully examined the dirty shirt. The pockets were empty, and it seemed very ordinary. Very dirty, but very ordinary.

The maid delivered the shirt to the cleaner, who really was the spy's partner. He immediately decoded a top-secret message.

How did the message get through? The spy had used the spaces between 26 lines on his striped shirt as an imaginary code strip. The soil spots were, in fact, the ink spot code on a shirt instead of a piece of paper!

Clever, huh?

The Picket Fence Code

A tall picket fence is a good way to keep out unwelcome snoops. And for writing secret messages, the picket fence code works exactly the same way. It completely shuts out nosy spies. Only your fellow Codemasters know how to "enter."

Here is how the picket fence code works. Suppose you want to send this urgent notice:

MEET ME IN THE PARK

First count the number of letters. Fifteen, right? Whenever you get an odd number, add a dummy letter at the end. You always want to work with an even number. Add an **X** to make 16 letters.

Now, copy your message on two lines in this special way: Place the first letter on the top line; put the second letter on the bottom line, one space to the right of the first letter.

Continue this way, placing a letter on the top line, then the bottom, then the top again, until you've written the whole message. If you link the top and bottom letters with lines, they will look like this:

MEMITEAK
ETENHPRX

The letters zigzag just like an old picket fence! Now you know how the code got its name.

Next, copy the top line of letters and then the bottom line in a row:

MEMITEAKETENHPRX

There! The message looks confusing already. To make the code even harder to break, divide the message into groups of three, four, or five letters:

MEM ITEA KETEN HPRX

Now you can send your secret message to a friend. To unscramble the code, all your friend has to do is repeat what you did, but backward.

First she counts the letters, but not the spaces, and draws a line that divides the code exactly in half:

MEM ITEA K/ETEN HPRX

Then she rewrites only the letters to the left of the line. Below that, she writes the letters to the right of the line:

MEMITEAK
ETENHPRX

Then she recopies the letters on a single line, taking one letter from the top line, then one from the bottom, then one from the top, and so on:

MEETMEINTHEPARKX

It is easy for your friend to guess where the spaces go between words. All she has to do is break up the line into words that make sense. She will know that there might be a dummy letter at the end.

Now that you have the hang of it, see if you can figure out the title of the famous book written below in picket fence code.

But watch out! A clever twist has been added — a trick that you can use, too. The message is written in cursive with some fake punctuation marks to fool you.

Tesr iln, Raue sad?

Use the picket fence code for your next hidden message. And if a curious spy tries to "break through" the secret writing, it will stop him right in his tracks. Just like a picket fence!

If you got *Treasure Island* by Robert Louis Stevenson, you cracked the code. Now crack open the book. It's a classic.

A HAIRY MESSAGE

A Codemaster has to use his head to think up clever ways to send secret messages. He can even use someone else's head.

That's what happened around 500 B.C. Histiaeus, the ruler of a large city in ancient Greece, was trying to oust the Persians from his land.

While Histiaeus was away on an official visit, he needed to send a message back to his citizens. He wanted them to attack the Persians. But how could he get his message through safely? The enemy would be watching.

Then he got a brainstorm. Histiaeus shaved the head of a trusted slave who was with him. Then he tattooed a secret message on the man's bald scalp and signed it. All Histiaeus had to do was to wait for the man's hair to grow back.

When the slave crossed enemy lines, his head was shaved once again. Histiaeus's signed message gave orders to revolt.

It was a good thing the message didn't need to be sent overnight. There was no way Histiaeus could have coaxed the hair to grow faster!

The Brown Fox Code

Notice anything unusual about this sentence?

THE QUICK BROWN FOX
JUMPS OVER THE LAZY DOG.

Figure it out? If not, study all the different letters.

Surprise! This short sentence contains all the letters of the alphabet. And some letters, such as **O** and **U**, appear more than once.

Now that you know the secret, this sentence can be a great way to send hidden messages. It is called the brown fox code. Here is how it works. Write down a number underneath each word:

```
THE  QUICK  BROWN  FOX
 1     2      3     4
JUMPS  OVER  THE  LAZY  DOG
  5     6     7    8     9
```

To change a letter into the brown fox code, first find the word that contains it. Take the letter **N**, for example. It is in the third word, **BROWN**. So write down the number **3**.

Next, count the position within the word that has the letter. **N** is the fifth letter of the word **BROWN**, so write the number **5** next to the **3**.

The letter **N** is coded as **35**.

It's that simple!

Try coding another letter. How about **S**?

It would be written as **55**. Pretty clever, isn't it?

Because some letters in the brown fox code appear more than once, you can really confuse a snoopy spy. Just choose different code numbers every time the same letter is used.

For example, an **O** in your secret message can be coded as **33** the first time and **61** when you use it again.

Here is one way to write the message **YOU ARE BEING FOLLOWED** in brown fox code:

843352 823273 3163233593 4161818142341391

Notice that the numbers in each word run together. So first you have to break them into pairs before unscrambling the code.

Now that you have the hang of it, try to figure out this book title:

**5384 55239163 6141 711273
5342223511822335**

You are sure to fool an undercover spy with the brown fox code. And your code friends will think it's fun and clever.

They might even think you are sly... like a fox!

It is *My Side of the Mountain* by Jean Craighead George.

The Curveball Code

If you like tossing a baseball, there is one pitch to save for just the right situation. It is sure to throw off even the most powerful slugger.

The ball swerves in such an unbelievable way that it looks like an optical illusion. You guessed it. It is a curveball. And it is never what it seems to be.

This is just how the curveball code works. It is sprinkled with meaningless letters to "throw off" everyone but your special code buddies. The fake letters will mislead a spy snoop in the same way that a curveball fakes out a batter.

The curveball code takes many forms. The easiest is to write out a message and then place a dummy letter (curveball) between each real one.

Suppose you want to send the message **CHANGE PASSWORD** in curveball code.

To disguise it, simply insert a fake letter in between the real ones:

CEHWAONUGLEZ PVAESJSFWHOQRTD

Since the new message has only twice as many letters as the original, it is a quick way to code urgent information.

Just like a curveball twists and turns, there are many variations to the curveball code. To disguise your message so it is harder to crack, make it every third letter. And if you want to be really tricky, include dummy numbers as well:

Z4C6SH3DAV8N5YGE2E4T
P7QA2CSW9SIXWU6O5TRA7D

You and your friend will have decided ahead of time how many dummy letters and numbers are between the real letters of your message. When he receives the message, he simply crosses out the fake "curveballs":

Z4C6SH3DAV8N5YGE2E4T
P7QA2CSW9SIXWU6O5TRA7D

There! You have thrown a curveball again. The message is the same as the one in the first code.

Another kind of curveball code reads like an innocent paragraph. Suppose a friend slipped you this note:

HAVING TROUBLE ABOUT LOUDSPEAKER. BELIEVE ANTENNA CONNECTED IMPROPERLY, BUT DO WHATEVER YOU CAN.

No, you do not cross out fake letters. Instead, read the last letter of each word. The message says:

GET READY TO RUN

MYSTERY BOOK

Now it is your turn at bat. First take a few practice swings. Then figure out the title of this book. The secret is to use every third letter.

PNT3KHZME BASHLE4SCOGR5AEFIT
JNGYKA7TREPD8BECKN

Did you get the title? Then congratulate yourself. You're batting a thousand!

SHERLOCK HOLMES
CLOBBERS A CURVEBALL

Sherlock Holmes, the fictional detective, was a first-rate code cracker. In one of his famous cases, he discovered a note that he believed contained a hidden code. The message read:

The supply of game for London is going steadily up. Head keeper Hudson, we believe, has been now told to receive all orders for fly paper and for preservation of your hen pheasant's life.

For several frustrating hours, Holmes tried to unravel the message. Finally he got it. Holmes began with the first word, *"The,"* and counted every third word after it. The secret message was: *The game is up. Hudson has told all. Fly for your life.*

The curveball code "strikes" again!

The Pyramid Code

Sometimes you're up against a truly brainy spy. How can a Codemaster confuse this sharp snoop?

One way would be to use a different code each time you write the same letter of the alphabet. If the letter **A** is coded **ML** in one word of a message and **FL** in another, it makes the code harder to crack.

All you need is the pyramid code. It looks like this:

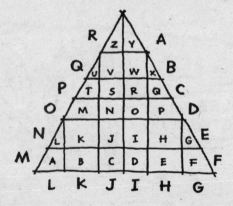

There are 26 letters in separate spaces inside the pyramid. These are the letters you want to disguise. In addition, the letters **A** through **R** go around the outside of the pyramid.

Now you have a complete key for passing along secret messages in pyramid code.

To change the letter **N** to pyramid code, first notice the letter outside the pyramid on the left that is in the same *row* as **N**. The letter is an **O**. Next, look for the letter underneath the pyramid that is in the same *column* as **N**. It's a **J**.

The letter **N** is written as **OJ**.

There is another way to code the letter **N**. Instead of using the letter **O** from the left side of the row, use the letter **D** from the right side. This time the letter **N** is coded as **DJ**.

Can you think of two more ways to send the letter **N**? It's easy! Just reverse the pair of letters. So an **N** can be written as:

OJ   **JO** (reversed)
DJ   **JD** (reversed)

Now let's write the message **BE CAREFUL** in pyramid code:

KM FH JM ML IC HM GF BK LN

Or, just to be tricky, run the pairs of letters together:

KMFHJMMLICHMGFBKLN

Make sure the person who gets the message has the same pyramid code key. Then it will be easy to unscramble all the letters and read the secret.

Another neat thing about the pyramid code is that you can change the position of the outside letters every time you use it. This is one example:

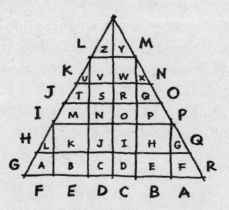

Now the letter **N** can be written as **ID**, **DI**, **PD**, or **DP**.

Use the pyramid code for all your top-secret messages. Decoding them really is a snap. Why, it's just as simple as A-B-C!

Would you like to test your skills with the pyramid code? See if you can figure out this book title using the pyramid from page 38.

EJIONHJOJDAIPKIPHMDKLFEIOJ

You have just decoded the classic *Johnny Tremain* by Esther Forbes.

The Double Dare Code

When you want to spy-proof an important secret message, the double dare code is one of the best codes to use.

The reason it is very tough to crack is that any letter can be coded in dozens of ways. Imagine that!

For example, the letter **H** can be coded as **15-12**, **23-12**, or **37-12**, to list just a few.

What's the secret? You need to use this double dare code chart. Study it carefully:

14	24	22	15	23	26	17	12	19	18	25	21	16
A	B	C	D	E	F	G	H	I	J	K	L	M
N	O	P	Q	R	S	T	U	V	W	X	Y	Z

Notice that the letters A to M are in the upper row and N to Z are in the lower row.

A line of numbers is above the letters. They are mixed up to make the chart completely spy-proof.

When you write a word, each letter is coded as two numbers. Now you know why it's called the double dare code! Here is an example:

27-14

The first number is called a *pointer*. It tells you whether the letter is in the upper row (A to M) or the lower row (N to Z) of the chart. Use any *odd* number as a pointer to show that the letter is in the upper row. In the example **27-14**, the number 27 "points" you to a letter in the upper row.

The second number in the code stands for the letter below that number. Look at the chart again. The letter **A** is in the upper row below the **14**. So the code **27-14** stands for the letter **A**.

OK so far? Notice the letter **N** is in the lower row. It also has a 14 above it. The pointer for a letter in the lower row will be an *even* number. Numbers such as 8, 72, and 64 "point" to letters in the lower row.

So the letter **N** can be coded as **28-14**, **36-14**, or **12-14**, among others.

Follow along as we disguise the word **SECRET** using the double dare code. One way would be:

14-26-25-23-37-22-18-23-23-23-16-17

Just to be tricky, you can skip a space in between the numbers, even if it "breaks" a letter in half:

14-26-25   23-37-22-18-23-23   23-16-17

Now that you have the hang of it, you are ready to write full sentences in double dare code. Use the number **00** to show your pal where one word ends and the next begins.

If you want to encode the message **GET HELP FAST**, it will look like this:

**39-17-15-23 14-17-00-29 12-17-23-37-21
34-22-00-19-26 27-14-16-26-22-17**

When your friend receives your message, he takes out his double dare chart. First he draws a circle around the twin zeros to show where the words end. Then he draws a line in between each set of two numbers:

39-17│15-23│ 14-17│(00)│29 12│17-23│37-21│

34-22│(00)│19-26│   27-14│16-26│22-17│

Now he writes the letter above each double set:

```
  G     E        T              H        E        L
39-17│15-23│  14-17│(OO)│29  12│17-23│ 37-21│

      P            F           A        S        T
  34-22│(OO)│19-26│   27-14│16-26│22-17
```

Your undercover message has arrived safely. Only your pal can figure it out! For your next message, you can make up your own chart using a different line of numbers.

Here is another chance to practice your double dare code skills. Try to figure out the title of this book:

16-24-34 14-00-17-16-22 21-00-15-12-28
24-22-14 38-24-12-23

You can even show a double dare message to a brainy spy and ask him to figure it out.

Go ahead, dare him. In fact...double dare him!

Finished? Then you should have unraveled *On My Honor* by Marion D. Bauer.

SWEATER SECRETS

Many years ago, secret agents used string and thread to send private messages. They sewed stitches in the pattern of embroidered clothing, then sent the clothing across enemy lines. The stitches turned out to be part of a special code.

At other times, an agent would send a friend a folksy letter that told how to design a sweater. The "friend" was actually a fellow agent. Once the friend finished knitting the sweater, its pattern would reveal a diagram of enemy positions.

But their enemies soon got suspicious. They hired a person to knit the sweater by following the letter's instructions. Imagine their surprise when the sweater turned out to be a map!

The Telephone Code

Did you know a secret message can be sent using the telephone? And you can do it without lifting the receiver.

How? The secret is hidden in the telephone's push buttons. That is why it is called the telephone code.

That's right! Almost all the letters of the alphabet are on the buttons.

A push-button phone looks like this:

If you want to write the letter **D** in telephone code, just look at each button. The letter **D** is above the number **3**. That means **3** is the code number for **D**.

So far, so good. But what about the letters **E** and **F**? They also are above the number **3**. How will your friend know which of the three letters you mean? All you need to do is follow this simple guide:

- If the letter is on the left, simply write down the number.
- If the letter is in the middle, write down the number and place a period after it.
- If the letter is on the right, write down the number and place a slash mark after it.

Here is how to code **D**, **E**, and **F** in telephone code:

- The code for **D** is **3**
- The code for **E** is **3.**
- The code for **F** is **3/**

Now let's try a sentence. Suppose you want to send the message **WE HAVE THURSDAY OFF** in telephone code. It will look like this:

93. 4.28/3. 84.8.7.7/329/ 6/3/3/

To make it even more confusing for a would-be spy, break up the numbers into different spacing:

93.4.2 8/3.84. 8.7.7/3 29/6/3/3/

Uh-oh. What about the letters **Q** and **Z**? They are missing from the push buttons. How can you code them?

Luckily, two push-button numbers, the **1** and **0**, do not have any letters. So the **1** can stand for **Q** and the **0** can stand for **Z**. The word **QUARTZ** would be written:

18.27.80

Ready for some practice? Write the message **CALL PAT NOW** in telephone code. After you do, check the solution below.

The message should read:

2/25/5/ 728 6.6/9

When your partner receives the message, he draws a push-button diagram and quickly decodes the sentence. If he forgets what the numbers mean, he can easily check a nearby telephone for help.

Now that you know how easy it is to use the telephone code, try out your skills and discover the title of this book. But be careful. Don't be fooled by the change in spacing or you will get the "wrong number."

86/5. 4/5/5/2 66/2/5.4/ 6.42.4/7.3

The next time you send a code to your friend, tell him you have a phone message for him. Then hand him a slip of paper in telephone code. He will figure out exactly what you mean!

You have just decoded *To Kill a Mockingbird* by Harper Lee.

The Ogham Code

One of the first codes ever used was invented by a tribal people known as the Celts. Centuries ago, they lived in western Europe and were known for their love of liberty and their sense of humor.

The Celtic code was called ogham (pronounced **ah**-gum). It looked like a bunch of scratchy lines.

Today, stone monuments bearing mysterious marks carved in ogham can be seen in Ireland and Wales.

The Celtic alphabet had 20 letters, and the ogham code looked like this:

AOUE IHDTC QBLVS NMGNGF R

The first group of lines crosses through a long center line. The second group of lines is above the center line, and the third is below it. The last group crosses the center line at a slant.

With a bit of imagination, you can figure out an expanded ogham code for use with our 26-letter alphabet. Here is the English version of ogham code:

ABC D E FGH I JKLM N OPQR S T U/VWX Y Z

We simply slanted the symbols in the last group in the opposite direction to represent the six additional letters in our alphabet. (Letters **U** and **V** share a symbol.)

It's a very neat-looking code. Notice that the last letter in each group (**E, J, O, T,** and **Z**) has its fifth line cutting across the other four.

If you want to send the letter **D** in ogham code, it will look like this:

To send the message **MEET AT NOON** in ogham code, first draw a long horizontal line across a piece of paper. Then draw the vertical lines for each letter:

Are you ready to decipher a secret ogham code message? It's the title of a classic book. Check it out:

Now you can send secret messages in one of the oldest codes known, just as the Celts did in Ireland. And that's no blarney!

If you decoded *The Call of the Wild* by Jack London, you've got it.

THE INVISIBLE MESSAGE

A windowpane can be used to send secret information. But the message will be invisible to everyone but you and your friend.

Simply write on the pane with your finger. The traces of oil from your finger cannot be seen.

To read the message, your friend breathes heavily on the window to fog it over. The message suddenly pops up, and it slowly fades as the moisture from his breath disappears.

Just like magic!

The Scramble Code

Do you know how to make scrambled eggs? Just crack them into a bowl, mix them up, and pour them into a heated skillet. When they are ready to eat, one egg is jumbled in with the other, just like a giant blob.

This is the same idea behind the scramble code. The letters are all there. But the words seem impossible to pick out.

Here is an interesting message in scramble code. How can you rearrange the letters to make sense?

**IAAFE RRTD SRNHLE IWKEEE HYWOW
VNOE NDO MEI**

Every word from your pal's message is included.

To unscramble a scramble code, first draw a line after every 12 letters. You can ignore the spaces between the words.

Then, for each group of 12 letters, draw three boxes like this. Notice that each box has four triangles:

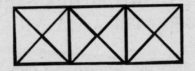

Suppose the message has 36 letters (that is, three sets of 12 letters), as in the one above. You draw three sets of boxes, one below the other.

Next, transfer the coded message, writing each letter inside a triangle.

But wait! Here is the tricky part of the scramble code. Print the letters from *top to bottom*, one column at a time. When you fill up the boxes, they will look like this:

Can you figure out the secret message? Read carefully from left to right, one row at a time.

Suddenly the secret writing begins to make sense. In fact, it jumps right out at you!

FINISH HOMEWORK EARLY.
WE RENTED A NEW VIDEO.

Cool, isn't it? What begins as a bunch of jumbled letters quickly becomes simple to read. That's why the scramble code is a good way to send a long message.

Making up a disguised note is just as easy as "cracking" it. Follow these simple steps:

- ✍ Write out your message.
- ✍ Divide it into groups of 12 letters (if the last group has fewer than twelve letters, add fake ones).
- ✍ Make up a row of three boxes for each group of 12 letters.
- ✍ Print the letters across in the triangles.
- ✍ Rewrite the letters on a sheet of paper by copying from *top to bottom* of each column. Add spacing wherever you choose.

There! Your coded message is complete.

Do you think you have the hang of it? Then pick up a pencil and paper and write this in scramble code:

MY DOG IS GUARDING OUR CLUBHOUSE

Finished? Your filled-in boxes should look like this:

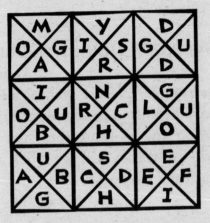

And this will be your coded message:

OOAM AIBUG GUBIRCY RNHSH SCD GLED DGOEI UUF

With a little practice you can become a scramble code pro. Then it should be easy for you to crack the title of this book:

ELT SVBSA FN AIEC RD OSLLR DMA

Use the scramble code for writing in your diary. Its secrets are safe even from a nosy spy. She could spend hours trying to figure out how the letters string together. But they will seem like one big blob.

Just like scrambled eggs!

Did you get it? The book is *Tales from Silver Lands* by Charles J. Finger.

The Split-Letter Code

Need an amazing code that is almost impossible to crack? Try the split-letter code. It is a perfect way to send top-secret messages.

These are the letters of the alphabet written in split-letter code:

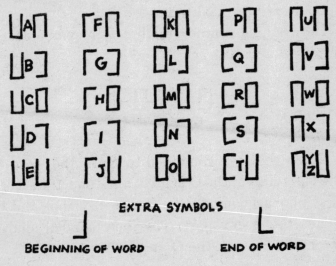

EXTRA SYMBOLS

BEGINNING OF WORD   END OF WORD

Now you know how the split-letter code got its name. Each letter in the alphabet chart is made up of two symbols.

How does the split-letter code work? It's really tricky. When you code a word, the right-hand symbol of the first letter is joined to the left-hand symbol of the letter next to it.

Here is an example, starting with symbols for the letters **O** and **N**:

$$\square\sqcup \quad \square\urcorner$$
O   **N**

When they are combined to make the word **ON**, the right half of the **O** symbol and the left half of the **N** symbol are joined to form a new symbol. But here comes the tricky part. This new symbol shares a common line with the **O** and **N**:

There! You have just learned how to write the word **ON** in split-letter code.

Get the idea? Now that you know how it works, get ready to try a longer word.

But first notice the extra symbols in the alphabet chart:

BEGINNING OF WORD   END OF WORD

They are used at the beginning and end of each word.

Here is how to write the word **CODE**. Follow along step by step:

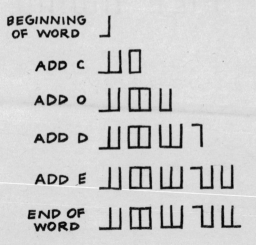

BEGINNING OF WORD

ADD C

ADD O

ADD D

ADD E

END OF WORD

When a friend gets your top-secret message, she takes out her alphabet chart and decodes it in a flash. As she unscrambles each pair of symbols, she inserts the letter in the space between them:

꜒c꜍꜏o꜎꜏꜍ᴅ꜒ᴇ꜏꜏

Now it is your turn to try the split-letter code. Are you ready?

Write the word **TRICKY** in split-letter code. Be sure to start out slowly. After carefully drawing the first few symbols, you will pick up speed in no time at all.

Finished? Then check out your message. It should look like this:

꜓ ꜖꜏ ꜍꜏ ꜎꜏ ꜌꜍ ꜍ᴏ꜍ ꜍꜏꜏

Now that you know how to convert a word into the split-letter code, try to decode the title of this book:

ЛГГ ⊏ Ш Ц

⊏ ⊏ Ш Г ⅃

A neat thing about the split-letter code is that you can create hundreds of different symbols just by combining halves of letters. It is all done with the simple alphabet chart.

What if an outsider accidentally discovers your alphabet chart? Don't worry. He will find it impossible to match up any of the symbols with the coded message.

A spy soon will give up in frustration on the split-letter code. Don't be surprised if he splits!

You have just decoded *White Stag* by Kate Seredy.

SECRETS IN YOUR DRAWER

A desk drawer is a neat place to hide secret papers. You can even use it for hiding small objects such as cassette tapes.

Some drawers have a space between the rear of the drawer and the chest it slides into. Attach the object *behind* the drawer. But be careful that the drawer doesn't stick out when you close it.

If you can't find a small space at the rear, use the *underside* of the drawer. It's a sneaky place to tape papers.

Even if someone were to open the drawer, your hiding place wouldn't be discovered.

The Knot Code

Do you like tying different kinds of knots?

If you do, you will want to use the knot code to send secret messages. It's a cool way to contact members of your secret club.

The knot code is simply Morse code in disguise. It's hidden on a string. One kind of knot stands for a dot and another kind for a dash.

For example, a dot can be an overhand knot, and a dash can be a figure eight:

Even if a snoopy spy finds the knotted string, he will never suspect it carries a hidden message.

This is the international Morse code for you to use:

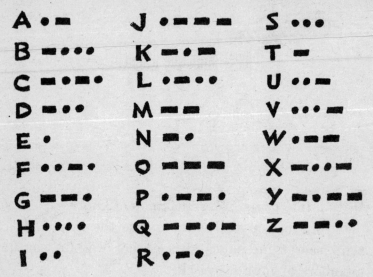

A •▬	**J** •▬▬▬	**S** •••
B ▬•••	**K** ▬•▬	**T** ▬
C ▬•▬•	**L** •▬••	**U** ••▬
D ▬••	**M** ▬▬	**V** •••▬
E •	**N** ▬•	**W** •▬▬
F ••▬•	**O** ▬▬▬	**X** ▬••▬
G ▬▬•	**P** •▬▬•	**Y** ▬•▬▬
H ••••	**Q** ▬▬•▬	**Z** ▬▬••
I ••	**R** •▬•	

To make the letter **A** in knot code, first tie an overhand knot near the left end of the string. But don't make it too tight. Next to it tie a figure eight knot. That's dot-dash, or **A**.

When you are ready to make the next letter, leave some space before you begin.

Here is how to tie the word **MEET** in knot code:

You can wrap your knot code message around a stick, hang it on a bush, or even mail it in an envelope. It looks like an old, worn-out piece of string.

When your friend gets it, all he has to do is study each knot and write down whether it is a dot or a dash.

But how will your friend know which end of the string is the left end? If he holds the string backward, an **A** looks like an **N**.

To avoid this problem, use a "starter knot" at the beginning of your message. It marks the left end of the string.

The starter can be any other kind of knot you choose. For example, it can be two overhand knots, one tied on top of the other.

Are you ready to try your hand at the knot code? See if you can untangle the title of this book:

And here is another neat idea for the knot code. Use it for making a bracelet with your club's password or your name. You can even knot the name of a person you secretly admire. No one will ever know!

If you know your knots, you figured out *The Hobbit* by J. R. R. Tolkien.